NINJA DUAL COOKBOOK

Tasty British Style Ninja Foodi Air Fryer AF300UK Recipes With Pictures Using Metric Measurements

Air fryer

ZONE UK

AF300

With Pictures

Using European Measurements!

2022-2023

By: Kylie Hardy

Table Of Contents

Introduction: Master your Ninja Air Fryer!

Chapter 1: Breakfast Recipes

Awesome Breakfast Frittata..1
Spicy Breakfast Sausage..2
Turkey Sausage Links..3
Blueberry Muffins..4
Delicious Apple Dumplings..5
Beef Ham & Mozzarella Grilled Cheese...6
Awesome Sweet Potato Hash...7
Quick French Toast Sticks Recipe...8
French Toast In The Air Fryer..9
Easy Greek Frittata..10
Delicious Breakfast Potatoes...11
Quick Hard-Boiled Eggs..12
Tasty Baked Potatoes..13

Chapter 2: Main Dishes

Awesome Spanish Tortilla..14
Dark Chicken Breast..15
Rib-Eye Steak Recipe...16
Spinach & Feta Casserole...17
Tasty Meatloaf...18
Turkey Breast Recipe..19
Alone at Home Salmon Recipe..20
Tasty Lemon-Garlic Salmon..21
Steak & Portobello Mushrooms...22
Lamb Chops Recipe..23
Crispy Cajun Crab Cakes...24
Small Meatloaves..25
Easy Sourdough Bread..26
Spicy Salmon Recipe...27
Awesome Salmon Cakes In The Air Fryer....................................28
Roasted Veggies Recipe..29

Easy Spicy Bay Scallops Recipe..30
Asparagus & Mushrooms Recipe..31
Korean Chicken Wings..32
Delicious Chicken Fajitas Recipe..33
Tasty Steak for Fajitas..34
Crispy Cajun Fish Fillets..35
Sausage Patties Recipe..36

Chapter 3: Starters and Sides

Awesome Sweet and Spicy Roasted Carrots..............37
Aubergine Parmesan Recipe..38
Easy Pizza Dogs Recipe..39
Cannoli Recipe..40
Jalapeño Poppers Recipe..41
Crispy Coconut Shrimp Recipe..42
Apple Pies Recipe..43
Tasty Churros Recipe..44

Mozzarella Sticks Recipe...45
Easy Baked Pineapple Recipe..46
Tasty Potato Wedges..47
Delicious Stuffed Mushrooms Recipe..48
Roasted Almonds Starter..49
Spicy Wings...50
Awesome Lemon Pepper Shrimp Recipe......................................51
Easy Spicy Runner Beans Recipe..52
Rosemary Potato Wedges Recipe..53
Roasted Asparagus side dish...54
Crispy Donut Sticks...55
Crispy Truffle Fries Recipe...56
Asparagus Fries Recipe..57
Crispy Avocado Fries Recipe...58
Delicious Corn Nuts Recipe..59
Enjoyable Roasted Bananas..60
Easy Spicy Roasted Peanuts Recipe...61

GETTING TO KNOW YOUR AIR FRYER

MAX CRISP: Use this function if you want to cook frozen foods, Ex: chicken nuggets & French fries...
AIR FRY: Apply this cooking mode if you are a fan of crispiness and crunch with little to no oil in the food.
ROAST: This function will turn the Ninja into oven mode to use for tender meats and more.
REHEAT: Simply, this function allows to reheat pre-cooked food and give them a crispy results
DEHYDRATE: Use this function if you want to cook healthy snacks using fruits, meats or vegetables.
BAKE: This function is generally used to cook desserts and baked treats...

OPERATING BUTTONS

The button n°1 is to apply the cooking settings on the drawer on the left.
The button n°2 is to apply the cooking settings on the drawer on the right.
TEMP arrows: To choose or modify the temperature degrees even during the process.
TIME arrows: To set or modify the cooking time even during the process.

SYNC button: Select this option if you want that the cooking ends at the same time in both zones regardless of the difference in time settings.
MATCH button: This option allows you to apply all the zone 1 settings to zone 2.
START/STOP button: This button allows you to begin the cooking process after adjusting all the necessary settings.
Power button: To run the machine or turn it off.
STANDBY MODE: After ten mins with no interaction with the control panel, the machine enters the standby mode.
HOLD MODE: This mode will show up when you apply the SYNC option, to hold the zone that has already finished until the other zone finishes cooking so they end at the same time.

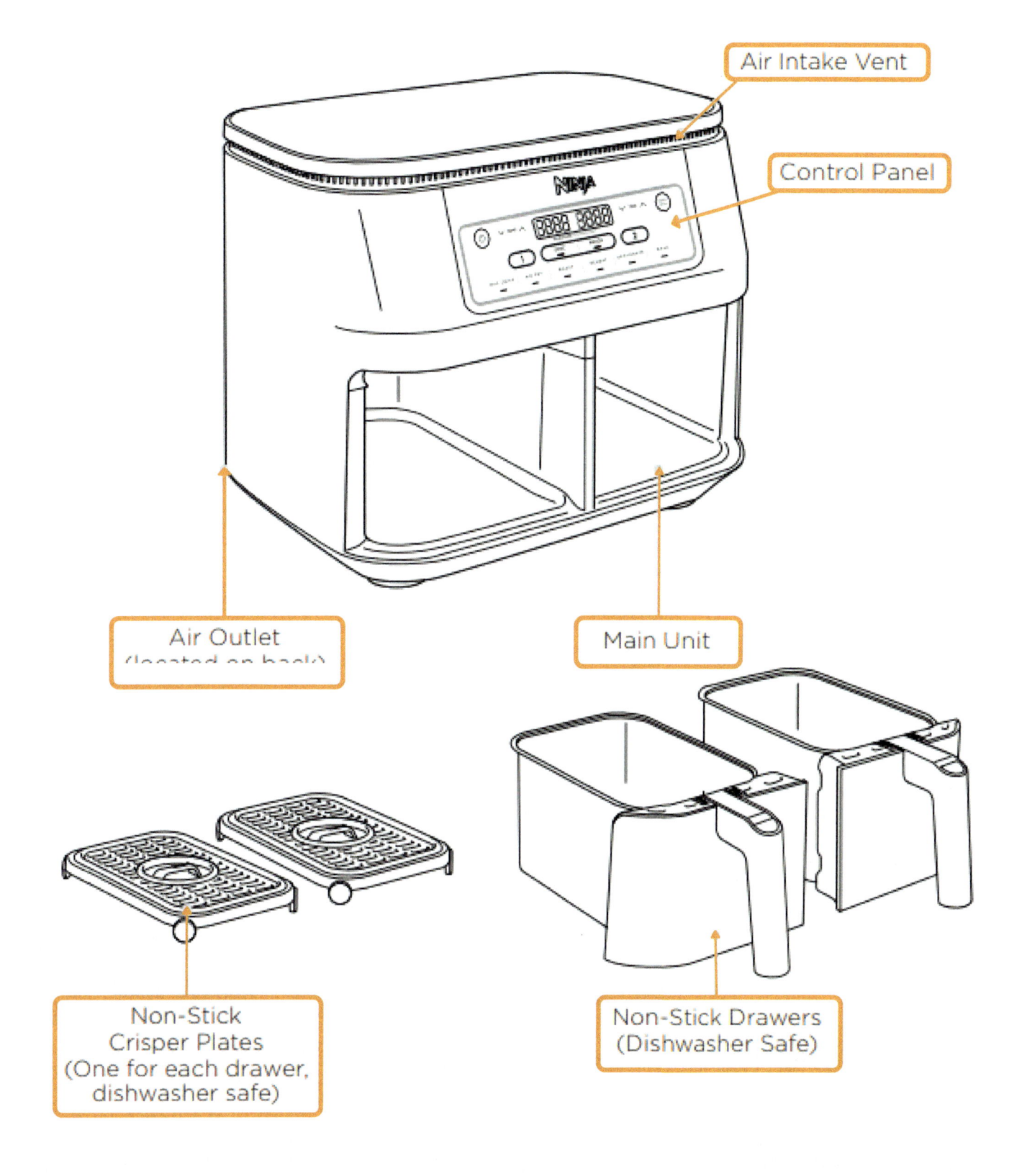

- Air Intake Vent
- Control Panel
- Air Outlet (located on back)
- Main Unit
- Non-Stick Crisper Plates (One for each drawer, dishwasher safe)
- Non-Stick Drawers (Dishwasher Safe)

THE STEP BY STEP GUIDE

SYNC

This option gives you the possibility if you want that the cooking ends at the same time in both zones regardless of the difference in time settings.

1. Add the components to the drawers, then insert drawers into the machine.

2. Zone 1 will stay illuminated. Choose the cooking mode that you want. Adjust the temp using the TEMP arrows, and set the cooking time using the TIME arrow.

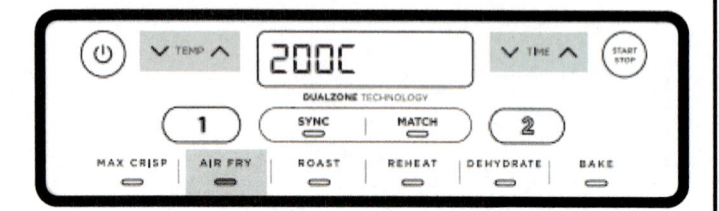

3. Choose Zone 2, then choose the cooking mode that you want. Adjust the temp using the TEMP arrows to set the temperature, and set the cooking time using the TIME arrow.

4. Select SYNC, then press the START/STOP button to start the process in the zone with the longest time. The second zone will be in **Hold** mode. The machine will beep and activate the second zone once both zones have the same time remaining.

NOTE: If you want to stop one zone before time ended, all you have to do is to select the concerned zone, then press START/STOP.

5. Once the cooking process ends, the machine will beep and "End" will show up on the display.

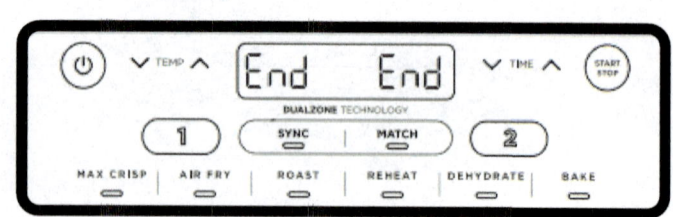

6. Transfer the ingredients from the drawer by tipping them out or using silicone-tipped tongs/utensils. **DON'T** put the drawer over the machine.

MATCH

This option allows you to apply all the zone 1 settings to zone 2.

1. Add the components to the drawers, then insert drawers into the machine.

2. Zone 1 will stay illuminated. Choose the cooking mode that you want. Adjust the temp using the TEMP arrows, and set the cooking time using the TIME arrow.

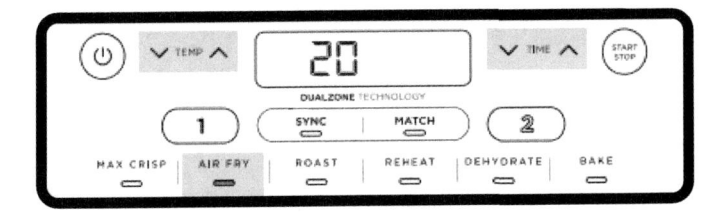

3. Select the **MATCH** mode to apply the settings of zone 1 to zone 2. Then press the START/ STOP button to start the process in both zones.

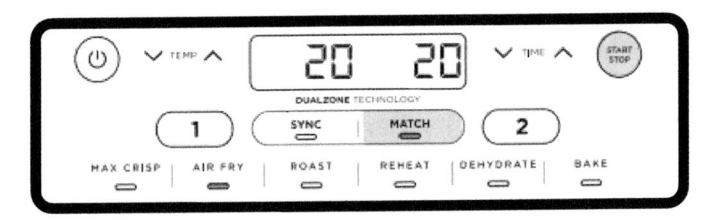

4. When the cooking process ends at the same time in both zones, "End" will show up on both screens.

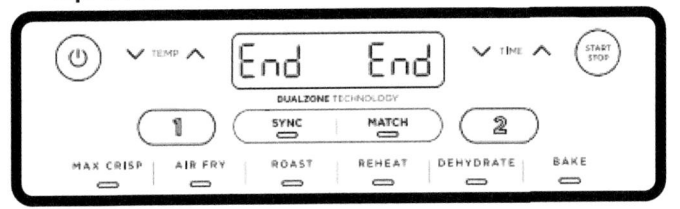

5. Transfer the ingredients from the drawer by tipping them out or using silicone-tipped tongs/utensils.

Starting both zones at the same time, but ending at different times:

1. Select Zone 1 and choose the cooking mode that you want. Adjust the temp using the TEMP arrows.

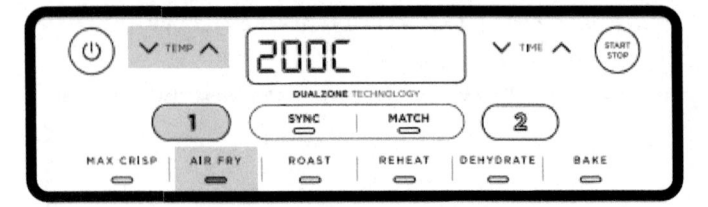

2. Set the cooking time using the TIME arrow.

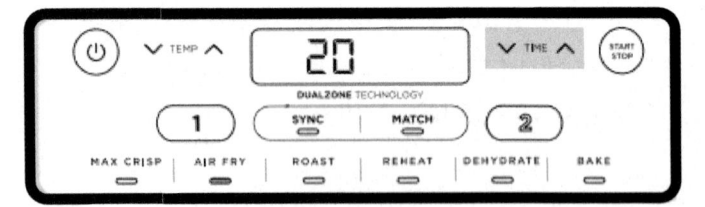

3. Choose zone 2 and apply the first and second step.

4. Select START/ STOP to start the process in both zones.

5. When the cooking process ends at the same time in both zones, "End" will show up on both screens.

6. Transfer the ingredients from the drawer by tipping them out or using silicone-tipped tongs/utensils.

Max Crisp

1. Put the crisper plate into the drawer, then add the ingredients to it, and insert the drawer into the machine.

2. The machine will automatically be set to zone 1 (to use zone 2, cheese zone 2). Press **MAX CRISP**.

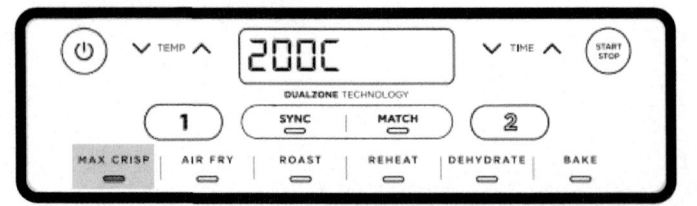

3. Set the cooking time using the TIME arrows in one min increments up to thirty mins. Press the START/STOP to start the process.

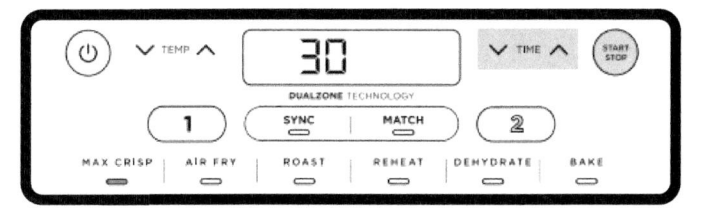

4. When the cooking process ends, "End" will show up on the display.

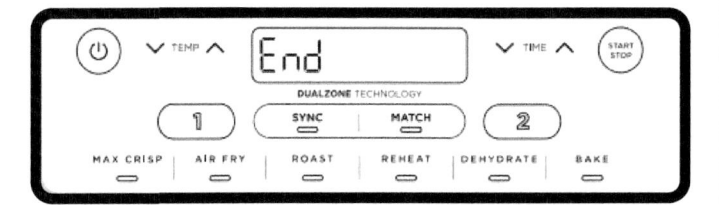

5. Transfer the ingredients from the drawer by tipping them out or using silicone-tipped tongs/utensils.

Air Fry

1. Put the crisper plate into the drawer, then add the ingredients to it, and insert the drawer into the machine.

2. The machine will automatically be set to zone 1 (to use zone 2, cheese zone 2). Press **AIR FRY**.

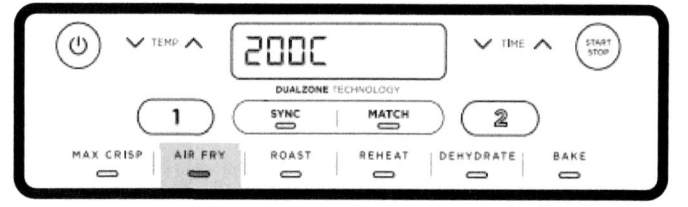

3. Adjust the temp using the TEMP arrows.

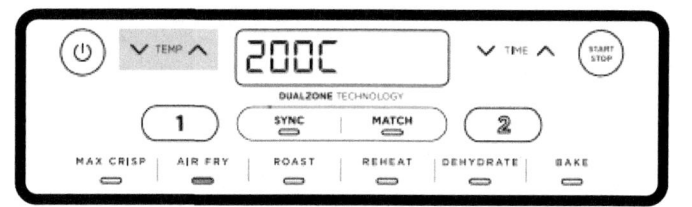

4. Set the cooking time using the TIME arrows in one min increments up to one hr. Press the START/STOP to start the process.

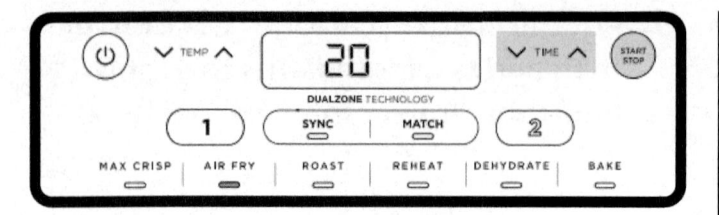

NOTE: While cooking, you can pull the drawer out of the unit and shake or toss the ingredients as mentioned in the recipes instructions.

5. When the cooking process ends, "End" will show up on the display.

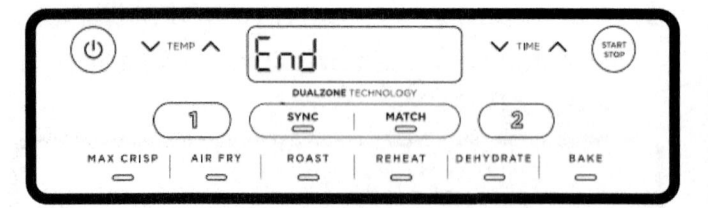

6. Transfer the ingredients from the drawer by tipping them out or using silicone-tipped tongs/utensils.

Roast

1. Put the crisper plate into the drawer (optional), then add the ingredients to it, and insert the drawer into the machine.

2. The machine will automatically be set to zone 1 (to use zone 2, cheese zone 2). Press **ROAST**.

3. Adjust the temp using the TEMP arrows.

4. Set the cooking time using the TIME arrows in one min increments up to five mins. Press the START/STOP to start the process.

Reheat

1. Put the crisper plate into the drawer (optional), then add the ingredients to it, and insert the drawer into the machine.

2. The machine will automatically be set to zone 1 (to use zone 2, cheese zone 2). Press **REHEAT**.

3. Adjust the temp using the TEMP arrows.

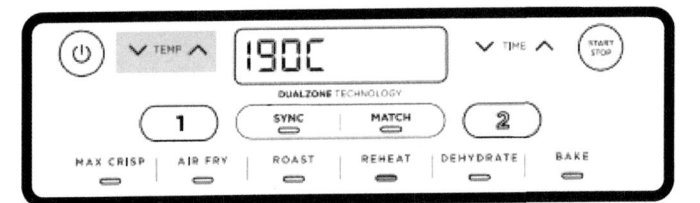

4. Set the cooking time using the TIME arrows in one min increments up to one hr. Press the START/STOP to start the process.

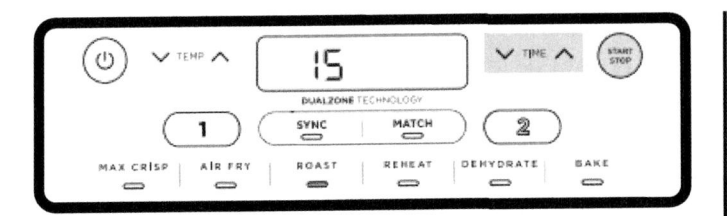

5. When the cooking process ends, "End" will show up on the display.

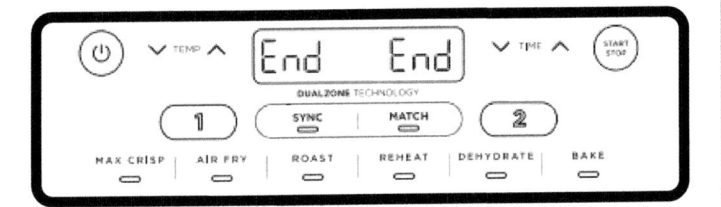

6. Transfer the ingredients from the drawer by tipping them out or using silicone-tipped tongs/utensils.

5. When the cooking process ends, "End" will show up on the display.

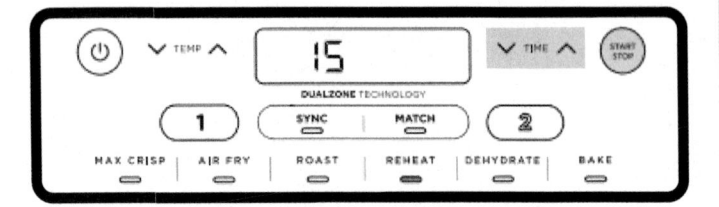

6. Transfer the ingredients from the drawer by tipping them out or using silicone-tipped tongs/utensils.

Dehydrate

1. Add one layer of components to the drawer. Then insert the crisper plate into the drawer over the components and add another layer of components to the crisper plate.

2. The machine will automatically be set to zone 1 (to use zone 2, cheese zone 2). Press **DEHYDRATE** and adjust the temp using the TEMP arrows.

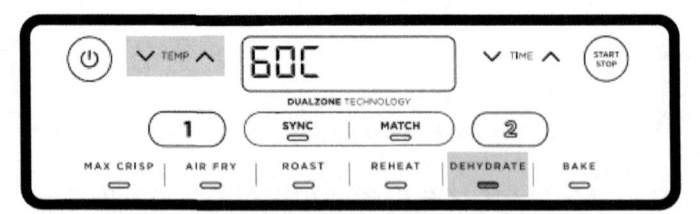

3. Set the cooking time using the TIME arrows in fifteen mins increments up to one to twelve hrs. Press the START/STOP to start the process.

4. When the cooking process ends, "End" will show up on the display.

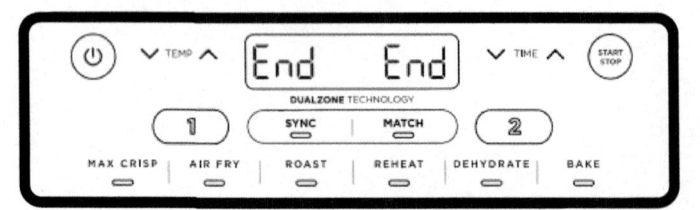

5. Transfer the ingredients from the drawer by tipping them out or using silicone-tipped tongs/utensils.

Bake

1. Put the crisper plate into the drawer (optional), then add the ingredients to it, and insert the drawer into the machine.

2. The machine will automatically be set to zone 1 (to use zone 2, cheese zone 2). Press **REHEAT**.

3. Adjust the temp using the TEMP arrows.

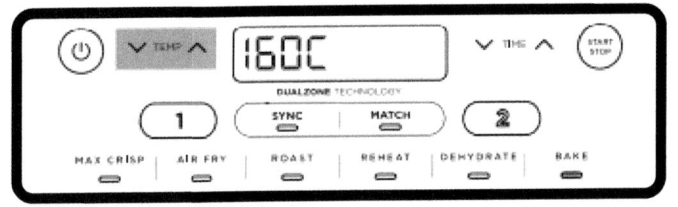

4. Set the cooking time using the TIME arrows in one min increments up to one to four hrs. Press the START/STOP to start the process.

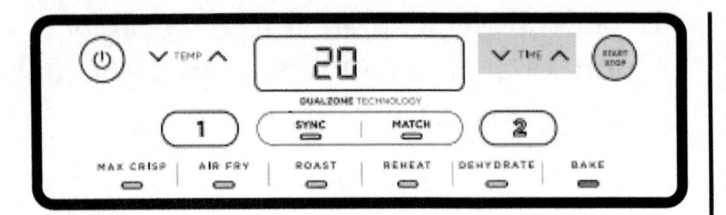

5. When the cooking process ends, "End" will show up on the display.

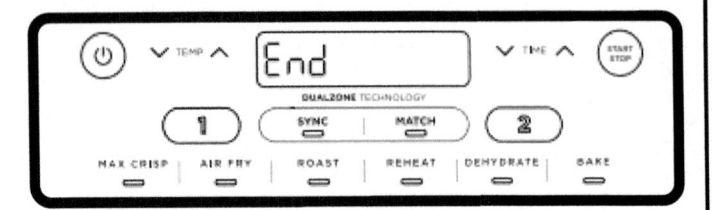

6. Transfer the ingredients from the drawer by tipping them out or using silicone-tipped tongs/utensils.

HELPFUL TIPS

1. Place all the ingredients in a layer on the bottom of the drawer without being covered by each other if you desire a consistent browning, and in case they are overlapping, you have to shake the drawer during the cooking process.
2. If you wanted to change the cooking time or the temperature while cooking, you will easily choose the concerned zone and then press the TIME or TIME arrows to make changes on them.
3. To make the recipes that you used to cook in your traditional oven, decrease the temp by 10°C and check food frequently to avoid overcooking.
4. Sometimes, the unit may blow lightweight foods around. If you want to avoid it, insert cocktail sticks on the top of your foods.
5. The crisper plate rises the components in the drawers whiches allows the air to go under and around components for even, crisp results.
6. After choosing the cooking mode you want, you can press the START/STOP button to start cooking right away, Because the unit will use the default temp & cook time.
7. To get better results when you cook fresh vegetables & potatoes, always add at least a tbsp of oil or even more to achieve the desired level of crispiness.
8. To get better results, remove food right away when the time ends to avoid overcooking.

CHAPTER 1

BREAKFAST RECIPES

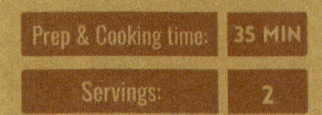

Awesome Breakfast Frittata

Prep & Cooking time: 35 MIN
Servings: 2

Ingredients

- 120g breakfast sausage fully cooked and crumbled
- Four eggs, beaten
- 120g Cheddar-Monterey Jack cheese blend, shredded
- 20g red pepper, diced
- One green onion, chopped
- cooking spray

Preperation

1. Mix the mentioned ingredients in a wide bowl and stir well, then preheat your NINJA FOODI DUAL ZONE AIR FRYER to 180°C.
2. Pick up the cooking spray and coat a nonstick cake pan that fits the drawer of your Ninja Air Fryer and transfer the mixture to it.
3. Place the pan into the drawer, and insert the drawer into the preheated unit. Zone 1, choose BAKE and cook for about eighteen to twenty min.

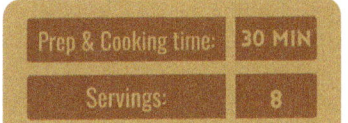

Spicy Breakfast Sausage

Prep & Cooking time: 30 MIN
Servings: 8

Ingredients

- 450g ground beef
- 5g sea salt
- 2g sage, rubbed
- 2g crushed red pepper
- 1g marjoram, dried
- 1g onion powder
- 1g ground black pepper
- 1g thyme, dried

Preperation

1. In the beginning, preheat your NINJA FOODI DUAL ZONE AIR FRYER to 200°C.
2. Mix the ground beef with the other mentioned ingredients in a wide bowl and combine well using your hands. Shape eight patties from the mixture.
3. Install a crisper plate in both drawers.
4. Divide the patties between the first and the second drawers of the NINJA DUAL ZONE. Insert the drawers and set Zone 1 to AIR FRY at 200°C. Set the time to five mins. Select the "MATCH" choice to apply the zone 1 settings to zone 2. Then press START/STOP to start.
5. Flip them and cook for five additional min. Serve!

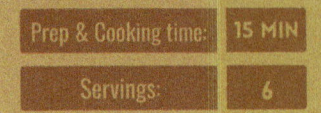

Turkey Sausage Links

Prep & Cooking time: 15 MIN
Servings: 6

Ingredients

- One (280g) pkg turkey breakfast sausage links

Preperation

1. In the beginning, preheat the NINJA FOODI DUAL ZONE AIR FRYER to 175°C.
2. Install the crisper plate in the drawer.
3. Place the sausage links into the drawer, and insert the drawer into the preheated unit.
4. The unit will default to zone 1, choose AIR FRY and cook for six mins.

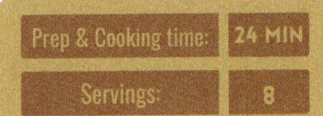

Blueberry Muffins

Prep & Cooking time: 24 MIN
Servings: 8

Ingredients

- 120g self-raising flour
- 30g white sugar
- 1g ground cinnamon
- 80ml milk
- 45g melted butter
- One egg
- 10ml vanilla extract
- 100g blueberries

Preperation

1. Preheat your NINJA FOODI DUAL ZONE AIR FRYER to 170°C for five mins.
2. Put the blueberries aside, mix the mentioned ingredients in a wide bowl and Blend well. Fold in blueberries. Divide the mixture among silicone cupcake liners.
3. Place the cupcake liners in the drawers of the NINJA DUAL ZONE, Insert the drawers into the unit, set Zone 1 to BAKE at 170°C and set the time to fourteen mins.
4. Select the "MATCH" choice to apply the settings of the first zone to the second zone. Then press START/STOP to start.

Delicious Apple Dumplings

Prep & Cooking time: 35 MIN
Servings: 8

Ingredients

- 30g raisins
- 15g Light brown sugar
- Two sheets of puff pastry
- Two small apples, peeled and cored
- 30g butter, melted

Preperation

1. In the beginning, preheat your Ninja Dual Zone Air Fryer to 180°C and use an aluminium foil to line one of the NINJA DUAL ZONE's baskets.
2. Combine raisins with sugar in a bowl.
3. Put one of those two sheets on a clean working board, place one apple on the sheet, and fill the core with raisins & sugar mixture. Fold the sheet to completely cover the apple.
4. Do it again with the other sheet, apple, and the rest of the raisins & sugar mixture.
3. Now, put both of them in the lined basket of your preheated machine and grease them with butter.
5. Insert the drawer into the preheated unit. The unit will default to zone 1, choose BAKE and cook for twenty-five mins.

Beef Ham & Mozzarella Grilled Cheese

Prep & Cooking time: 15 MIN
Servings: 1

Ingredients

- 30g unsalted butter, softened
- Two slices of sourdough bread
- 60g Beef ham
- 80g fresh mozzarella, sliced

Preperation

1. First, preheat your Ninja Dual Zone Air Fryer to 180°C.
2. Grease a bread slice with butter, and add beef ham & mozzarella.
3. Grease the other bread slice with butter, and close the sandwich. (The sides of bread that you've greased should be facing out)
4. Install the crisper plate in the drawer.
5. Put the sandwich into the drawer, and insert the drawer into the preheated unit. The unit will default to zone 1, choose AIR FRY and set the time to eight min. Press START/STOP to begin.

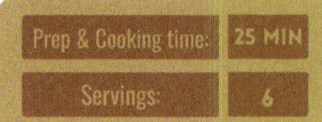

Awesome Sweet Potato Hash

Prep & Cooking time: 25 MIN
Servings: 6

Ingredients

- Two large sweet potatoes, cubed
- Two slices of smoked beef ham, cut into small pieces
- 30ml olive oil
- 2g smoked paprika
- 5g sea salt
- 2g ground black pepper
- 2g dill weed, dried

Preperation

1. Preheat the Ninja Dual Zone Air Fryer to 200°C.
2. Mix sweet potato, and beef ham with the other ingredients in a bowl.
3. Transfer everything to the drawer, and insert the drawer into the preheated unit.
4. Select the ROAST function, set the time to sixteen mins and press the START/STOP button to begin. Check and stir from time to time.

Quick French Toast Sticks Recipe

Prep & Cooking time: 20 MIN
Servings: 2

Ingredients

- Four slices of thick bread
- Parchment paper
- Two eggs, beaten
- 60ml milk
- 5ml vanilla extract
- 2g cinnamon

Preperation

1. Split the bread slices into three sticks. Put the parchment paper in the bottom of your Ninja Dual Zone Air Fryer drawers. Preheat to 180°C
2. In a bowl, pour milk and mix it well with the other ingredients except for the bread. Then, dredge the breadsticks in the mixture, Shake, and divide them between both prepared drawers.
3. Insert the drawers into the unit, set Zone 1 to AIR FRY and set the time to five mins.
4. Select the "MATCH" choice to apply the settings of the first zone to the second zone. Then press START/STOP to start. Flip, and cook for five min more.

French Toast In The Air Fryer

Prep & Cooking time: 20 MIN
Servings: 4

Ingredients

- Two eggs
- 80ml milk
- 15g salted butter, melted
- 15ml vanilla extract
- 2g ground cinnamon
- 4 slices of day-old bread
- 3g confectioners' sugar, or as you desire

Preperation

1. Except for the sugar, combine all the ingredients together in a bowl. Put parchment paper in the bottom of your machine's drawer and coat it with a nonstick cooking spray. Dredge the bread slices in the combine and put them separated in the prepared drawer.
2. Now, preheat your Ninja Dual Zone Air Fryer to 190°C.
3. Select ROAST and set the time to six mins. Then press START/STOP to start.
4. Turn them and cook for two to three additional min. Sprinkle with sugar and serve.

Easy Greek Frittata

Prep & Cooking time: 30 MIN
Servings: 2

Ingredients

- Four eggs
- 45g heavy whipping cream
- 10g coarsely chopped spinach leaves
- 100g feta cheese
- 100g cherry tomatoes, halved
- 30g red onion, diced
- 2g dried oregano
- Salt and freshly ground black pepper

Preperation

1. Preheat your Ninja Dual Zone Air Fryer to 175°C. Coat a cake pan that fits in the drawer with a nonstick spray.
2. Beat the eggs & cream in a bowl, add spinach, feta cheese, cherry tomatoes, onion, oregano, salt, and pepper, combine the mixture and transfer it to that cake pan and close it with a foil.
3. Place the pan into the drawer, and insert the drawer into the preheated unit. choose BAKE, set the time to twelve mins and press START/STOP to start.
4. Discard the foil and keep cooking for about four to eight min more to brown the top.

Delicious Breakfast Potatoes

Prep & Cooking time: 30 MIN
Servings: 2

Ingredients

- 450g peeled russet potatoes, cut into 1-inch cubes
- 15ml olive oil
- 5g salt
- 2g onion powder
- 2g paprika
- 0.5g ground black pepper

Preperation

1. Put the potatoes in a medium bowl, pour cold water over them until they are fully covered, and leave them for thirty mins.
2. Turn on your Ninja Dual Zone Air Fryer, set the temperature to 200°C and preheat it.
3. Meanwhile, drain the potatoes and pat dry them using a paper towel. pour olive oil over and add pepper, salt, paprika, and onion powder. Stir to combine with the potato cubes.
4. Transfer the potatoes to your Ninja Ninja Dual Zone Air Fryer Drawer and ROAST for twenty mins; shaking halfway through the cooking time.

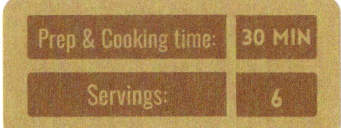

Quick Hard-Boiled Eggs

Prep & Cooking time: 30 MIN
Servings: 6

Ingredients

- Six eggs

Preperation

1. First, Install the crisper plate in the drawer and preheat your Ninja Dual Zone Air Fryer to 120°C.

2. Add the eggs to the drawer, Select BAKE and set the time to fifteen mins. Then, transfer them to cold water for eight to ten min to get cooled. Serve!

Tasty Baked Potatoes

Prep & Cooking time: 1 HR
Servings: 4

Ingredients

- Four large baking potatoes
- 30ml olive oil
- coarse sea salt
- ground black pepper
- garlic powder
- dried parsley
- 60g butter

Preperation

11. As a first step, preheat your Ninja Dual Zone Air Fryer to 200°C.
2. Grease potatoes with oil, and season with the remaining seasoning mentioned on the list.
3. Transfer them to the drawers of your preheated unit.
4. Insert the drawers into the unit, set Zone 1 to BAKE and set the time to fifteen mins.
5. Select the "MATCH" choice to apply the settings of the first zone to the second zone. Then press START/STOP to start.
6. Mince potatoes longwise. Stuff each potato with 15g of butter. Serve!

CHAPTER 2

MAIN DISHES

Lunch Dinner

Awesome Spanish Tortilla

Prep & Cooking time: 65 MIN
Servings: 4

Ingredients

- One large potato, peeled cubed
- 15ml extra-virgin olive oil
- 15g leek, sliced
- Five eggs
- 60g Pecorino Romano cheese, grated
- salt and ground black pepper
- 5g fresh flat-leaf parsley, chopped

Preperation

1. Put the potatoes in a large bowl. Pour cold water over them until they get covered, and leave them like that for ten min.
2. Next, preheat the Ninja Dual Zone Air Fryer to 160°C.
3. Place the potatoes in a bowl after draining them, pour oil, and mix. Transfer them to your machine's drawer and BAKE for eighteen min, then raise the heat to 180°C, Shake before and after adding leek slices, Cook for around three min.
4. Meantime, In a mixing bowl beat the eggs with cheese, salt, and pepper, mix well and pour the mixture into a nonstick cake pan. Add the potato cubes & leek to them.
5. Insert the pan into the drawer and set the time to fifteen mins. Then press START/STOP to start.
6. When it's done, cool for five min. Drizzle the parsley over and serve.

Dark Chicken Breast

Prep & Cooking time: 40 MIN
Servings: 2

Ingredients

- 5g paprika
- 2g ground thyme
- 3g cumin
- 3g cayenne pepper
- 3g onion powder
- 2g black pepper
- 2g salt
- 10ml vegetable oil
- Two (340g) skinless, boneless chicken breast halves

Preperation

1. Put the chicken and oil aside and mix the other ingredients in a small bowl, then put the mixture on a platter.
2. Grease the chicken with vegetable oil. Dredge the chicken in the combine you've just made, and coat them on all sides. Leave it for five min.
3. Meanwhile, preheat your Ninja Dual Zone Air Fryer to 175°C.
4. After the five min, Install the crisper plate in the drawer and put the chicken into it, Select AIR FRY, set the time to ten mins and press START/STOP to start.
5. Flip them and cook for ten mins more.

Rib-Eye Steak Recipe

Prep & Cooking time: 85 MIN
Servings: 2

Ingredients

- Two rib-eye steaks, cut into 3cm thick
- 15g grill seasoning
- 60ml olive oil
- 130ml reduced-sodium soy sauce

Preperation

1. Mix the steaks with the remaining ingredients in a large bowl, cover the bowl, and marinate the steaks for 120 min or even more.
2. Install the crisper plate in the drawer, and pour around 20ml water into the bottom of the drawer to avoid smoking while cooking meat. Then, preheat your Ninja Dual Zone Air Fryer to 200°C.
3. Pull out the meat from the bowl, discard the marinade and place it in the drawer, and insert the drawer into the preheated unit. Choose AIR FRY, set the time to seven mins and press START/STOP to start.
4. Flip and cook for seven additional min. Enjoy!

Spinach & Feta Casserole

Prep & Cooking time: 30 MIN
Servings: 4

Ingredients

- cooking spray
- One (50g) can of spinach, drained and squeezed
- 225g cottage cheese
- Two eggs, beaten
- 60g crumbled feta cheese
- 15g plain flour
- 30g butter, melted
- 1 clove of garlic, minced
- 5g onion powder
- 1g ground nutmeg

Preperation

1. First, you gotta preheat your Ninja Dual Zone Air Fryer to 190°C. Spray a pie pan with the cooking spray.
2. Combine all the ingredients in the list in a medium bowl. Mix them and pour the combine into the pan.
3. Place the pan in the drawer, and insert the drawer into the Ninja Dual Zone Air Fryer. choose BAKE, set the time to twenty mins and press START/STOP to start.

Tasty Meatloaf

Prep & Cooking time: 45 MIN
Servings: 4

Ingredients

- 450g lean ground beef
- One egg, lightly beaten
- 25g breadcrumbs
- One small onion, chopped
- 5g fresh thyme, chopped
- 5g salt
- ground black pepper to taste
- Two mushrooms, thickly sliced
- 15ml olive oil

Preperation

1. First, you gotta preheat your Ninja Dual Zone Air Fryer to 200°C.
2. In a large bowl, place all the ingredients except for the mushrooms and olive oil, and mix them thoroughly.
3. Place the combine in a baking pan that fits the drawer of the Ninja Foodi and spread it.
4. Add mushrooms to the top and pour the olive oil over to coat. Place the pan into the drawer.
5. Insert the drawer into the preheated unit. choose ROAST, set the time to twenty-five mins and press START/STOP to start. Serve after ten min of rest.

Turkey Breast Recipe

Prep & Cooking time: 1 HR
Servings: 6

Ingredients

- 5g finely fresh rosemary, chopped
- 2g fresh chives, chopped
- 3g fresh garlic, minced
- 3g salt
- 1g ground black pepper
- 30g cold unsalted butter
- 1.24kg skin-on, bone-in split turkey breast
- oms, thickly sliced
- 15ml olive oil

Preperation

1. Preheat the Ninja Dual Zone Air Fryer to 175°.
2. Place all the herbs and seasonings onto a cutting board. Slice the butter over them and mash until well blended.
3. Rub the dried turkey with the herbed butter you've just made even between the skin.
4. Now, transfer it to the drawer after installing the crisper plate, skin-side in the bottom, Select AIR FRY and cook for twenty min.
5. Flip and keep frying for around eighteen additional min. When it's done, place the meat on a plate and tent it with aluminium foil for ten min before serving.

Alone at Home Salmon Recipe

Prep & Cooking time: 20 MIN
Servings: 1

Ingredients

- 1 (170g) salmon fillet
- 2g salt
- 2g Greek seasoning
- 1g ground black pepper
- A pinch of dill weed, dried

Preperation

1. First, you have to preheat your Ninja Dual Zone Air Fryer to 190°C, for five mins.
2. Meantime, season the salmon with the herbs and seasonings you have on the list.
3. Put a perforated parchment round in the bottom of the Ninja drawer. Add the fillet inside, skin-side in the bottom, Select AIR FRY and cook for around fifteen min.

Tasty Lemon-Garlic Salmon

Prep & Cooking time: 25 MIN
Servings: 2

Ingredients

- 15g melted butter
- 2g garlic, minced
- Two (170g) fillets center-cut salmon fillets
- 1g lemon-pepper seasoning
- 0.5g dried parsley
- cooking spray
- Three thin lemons halved slices

Preperation

1. First, you have to preheat your Ninja Dual Zone Air Fryer to 200°C, for five min.
2. In a little bowl, mix the butter with garlic and use it to brush the dried salmon, drizzle lemon pepper, and parsley to season the fillets.
3. Install the crisper plate in the drawer, Coat it with cooking spray, Inset the fillets on it, skin-side in the bottom, and divide lemon slices on top of them. Choose AIR FRY and set the time to ten mins. Serve after two min of rest.

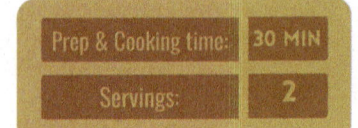

Steak & Portobello Mushrooms

Prep & Cooking time: 30 MIN
Servings: 2

Ingredients

- 60ml olive oil
- 15ml soy-free seasoning sauce
- 10g Montreal steak seasoning
- 1g garlic powder
- Two strip steaks, cut into 2cm pieces
- 120g portobello mushrooms, quartered

Preperation

1. Mix soy-free seasoning sauce, steak seasoning, olive oil, and garlic in a little bowl, put the steak pieces, in the mixture, and marinate for fifteen min.
2. Now, preheat your Ninja Dual Zone Air Fryer to 200°C.
3. Put a perforated parchment round in the bottom of your machine's Drawer.
4. Remove the steak pieces from the mixture. Place the drained steak with mushrooms in the Drawer.
5. Select ROAST and set the time to five mins, then pull the drawer out, toss, put it back into the unit and cook for four mins more.

Lamb Chops Recipe

Prep & Cooking time: 25 MIN
Servings: 4

Ingredients

- Four boneless, center-cut lamb chops, 2cm thick
- cooking spray
- 5g dry ranch salad dressing mix

Preperation

1. Put the lamb chops on a platter and spray them (all sides). Season lightly with the seasoning mix and leave it for ten min.
2. Install the crisper plate in the drawer, coat it with cooking spray and preheat to 200°C,
3. Put the lamb in the drawer of your preheated Ninja Dual Zone Air Fryer and cook for about five min. Then flip and cook for five additional min. Leave it on a foil-covered platter for five min. Serve!

Crispy Cajun Crab Cakes

Prep & Cooking time: 25 MIN
Servings: 3

Ingredients

- 90g panko breadcrumbs
- 60g mayonnaise
- One egg
- 10ml Worcestershire sauce
- 5g Dijon mustard
- 2g Cajun seasoning
- 3g salt
- 1g cayenne pepper
- 120g lump crabmeat
- 45g remoulade sauce

Preperation

1. First, you gotta preheat your Ninja Dual Zone Air Fryer to 190°C.
2. In a little bowl, place the ingredients except for the remoulade sauce & crabmeat and combine them, then fold in crabmeat.
3. Shape three crab cakes with a fit cutter. Put a perforated parchment round in the bottom of your machine's drawers.
4. Divide the cakes among zone 1 and zone 2. Insert the drawers into the unit, set Zone 1 to AIR FRY and set the time to six mins.
5. Select the "MATCH" choice to apply the settings of the first zone to the second zone. Then press START/STOP to start.
6. Flip and keep cooking for around six additional min. Serve with the sauce on your desired buns.

Small Meatloaves

Prep & Cooking time: 50 MIN
Servings: 6

Ingredients

- Cooking spray
- 900g ground chuck
- One egg
- 30g breadcrumbs, seasoned
- 30g mayonnaise
- 4g onion powder
- 5g salt
- 90g ketchup

Preperation

1. Install crisper plate in the drawer, grease the drawer with oil, then preheat to 200°C.
2. Combine all the ingredients except for the ketchup in a wide bowl, Shape six small loaves of the mixture.
3. Divide the meatloaves separated between zone 1 and zone 2. Insert the drawers into the unit, set Zone 1 to ROAST and set the time to thirty mins.
4. Select the "MATCH" choice to apply the settings of the first zone to the second zone. Then press START/STOP to start.
5. Divide the ketchup over them and cook for three additional min.

Easy Sourdough Bread

Prep & Cooking time: 5 HRS 30 MINS
Servings: 6

Ingredients

- 140g bread flour
- 60g spelled flour
- 100g sourdough starter
- 15ml extra-virgin olive oil
- 2g fine sea salt
- 100ml water

Preperation

1. In your stand mixer, mix the ingredients together without water, mix them with the dough hook, then pour water to combine the mixture, Keep kneading at low speed for around five min.
2. Shape a ball from the dough. put it in a baking dish that fits with the drawer of your Ninja Dual Zone Air Fryer, cover it with plastic wrap and leave it overnight.
3. Nex, preheat your Ninja Dual Zone Air Fryer to 200°C.
4. Discard the wrap and scratch the dough. Place the dish in the drawer and insert the drawer into the unit.
5. Select the BAKE function, set the time to twenty mins and press START/STOP to start cooking.

Spicy Salmon Recipe

Prep & Cooking time: 25 MIN
Servings: 6

Ingredients

- 10g grill seasoning
- 13g Light brown sugar
- 2g ground cumin
- 2g ground coriander
- 1g cayenne pepper
- 900g salmon fillets, skin on

Preperation

1. First, preheat your Ninja Dual Zone Air Fryer to 165°C for two min.
2. Mix all the seasoning in a little bowl. Sprinkle some of it over each fillet.
3. Transfer the fillets to your preheated machine's drawer and cook them on the AIR FRY mode for around eighteen min. Serve it warm!

Awesome Salmon Cakes In The Air Fryer

Prep & Cooking time: 20 MIN
Servings: 4

Ingredients

- A large egg
- 30g mayonnaise
- 4g fresh parsley, chopped
- 4g fresh chervil, chopped
- 4g fresh dill, chopped
- 3g fresh chives, chopped
- 3ml Worcestershire sauce
- 3g Dijon mustard
- 3g seafood seasoning
- 3g salt
- 30g panko breadcrumbs
- Two (140g) pkg of salmon, fresh

Preperation

1. Preheat your Ninja Dual Zone Air Fryer for ten min to 200°C.
2. Put the breadcrumbs & salmon aside and whisk the egg with the other ingredients together in a medium bowl, then combine with the breadcrumbs and fold in the salmon.
3. Form four equal cakes of the combine.
4. Install the crisper plate in the drawer, and put a perforated parchment in the bottom of the drawer.
5. Place the salmon cakes inside, Set the Ninja Dual Zone Air Fryer to AIR FRY mode, and the time to eight mins, turning to both sides during the cooking time. Serve immediately.

Roasted Veggies Recipe

Prep & Cooking time: 30 MIN
Servings: 4

Ingredients

- 70g courgette, diced
- 70g summer squash, diced
- 70g mushrooms, diced
- 70g cauliflower, diced
- 70g asparagus, diced
- 70g sweet red pepper, diced
- 10ml vegetable oil
- 1g salt
- 1g ground black pepper
- 1g seasoning

Preperation

1. First, you gotta preheat your Ninja Dual Zone Air Fryer to 180°C.
2. In a wide bowl, mix all the ingredients together, toss, and place everything in your preheated machine's drawer after Installing the crisper plate.
3. Cook for ten mins on ROAST cooking mode, stirring after five mins. Serve!

Easy Spicy Bay Scallops Recipe

Prep & Cooking time: 15 MIN
Servings: 4

Ingredients

- 450g bay scallops, rinsed and patted dry
- 5g smoked paprika
- 5g chili powder
- 5ml olive oil
- 2g garlic powder
- 1g ground black pepper
- 0.5g cayenne red pepper

Preperation

1. In the first step, preheat your Ninja Dual Zone Air Fryer to 200°C.
2. Mix all the ingredients together, toss.
3. Place everything in your preheated machine's drawer.
4. Set the Ninja Dual Zone Air Fryer to AIR FRY mode, and the time to eight mins, shake the basket during cooking. Serve!

Asparagus & Mushrooms Recipe

Prep & Cooking time: 25 MIN
Servings: 2

Ingredients

- 225g bay scallops, rinsed and patted dry
- Eight spears asparagus, trimmed and cut into 2cm pieces
- Four medium mushrooms, sliced
- 15ml olive oil
- 3g lemon-pepper seasoning
- 2g parsley flakes
- 1g ground paprika
- Two lemon wedges

Preperation

1. First, you gotta preheat your machine to 200°C,
2. In a large bowl, mix all the ingredients together except for the lemon wedges, and toss.
3. Place everything in your preheated Ninja Dual Zone Air Fryer drawer, ROAST for around eight mins, and shake during cooking. Serve with the wedges!

Korean Chicken Wings

Prep & Cooking time: 40 MIN
Servings: 2

Ingredients

- 80ml reduced-sodium soy sauce
- 50g Light brown sugar
- 30g Korean hot pepper paste
- 5ml sesame oil
- 2g ginger paste
- 1g garlic paste
- Two green onions, chopped
- 450g chicken wings
- 5ml vegetable oil

Preperation

1. Preheat your Ninja Dual Zone Air Fryer to 200°C.
2. In a medium pan, mix all the ingredients together except for the chicken & vegetable oil and boil the mixture over medium-high heat, then simmer it to get thickened, around four mins.
3. In a wide bowl, put the chicken, pour the vegetable oil over it and rub the wings to coat.
4. Install the crisper plates in the drawers.
5. Divide wings between the drawers of your preheated machine. Select the MAX CRISP function and set the time to ten mins.
6. Select the "MATCH" choice to apply the settings of the first zone to the second zone. Then press START/STOP to start.
7. Flip and cook for ten additional mins.
8. Dip the wings in the combine you've made in the first step, then add them back to the drawers and cook for two further mins.
9. Dredge wings into the combine another time, add them back to the Ninja Dual Zone Air Fryer drawers and cook two min more. Serve immediately!

Delicious Chicken Fajitas Recipe

Prep & Cooking time: 50 MIN
Servings: 8

Ingredients

- One medium red pepper, strips
- One medium green pepper, strips
- One onion, sliced
- 15ml olive oil, divided
- salt and pepper to taste
- 450g chicken tenders, strips
- 5g fajita seasoning
- Eight flour tortillas, warmed

Preperation

1. In a wide bowl, put the peppers & onion. Pour 10ml of olive oil and add salt and pepper. Stir.
2. In another bowl, put the chicken and season with fajita seasoning.
3. Pour the rest of the olive oil and combine well. Next, Install the crisper plate in the drawer and preheat your Ninja Dual Zone Air Fryer to 175°C, Place the chicken in the drawer and AIR FRY for about twelve min, shake it during cooking.
4. Then, place it on a platter until you cook the first mixture.
5. Now, place the combine you've made in the first step in the drawer and cook for around fourteen min, shaking during cooking. Divide everything between tortillas and serve.

Tasty Steak for Fajitas

Prep & Cooking time: 8 HRS 30 MINS
Servings: 4

Ingredients

- 1g ground coriander
- 10g salt
- 1g garlic powder
- 30ml olive oil
- 1g ground cumin
- 45g skirt steak, strips
- One onion, strips
- One red pepper, strips

Preperation

1. Mix all the herbs & seasoning in the list in a resealable plastic bag, then add the rest of the ingredients to the bag and combine them.
2. Close your bag and put it in the refrigerator overnight.
3. Put a perforated parchment paper in the Ninja Dual Zone Air Fryer drawer.
4. Take off the meat, peppers, and onions from the packet and add them to the prepared drawer.
5. ROAST for five min at 200°C, Shake the basket and cook for around four min until it's completely cooked.

Crispy Cajun Fish Fillets

Prep & Cooking time: 25 MIN
Servings: 4

Ingredients

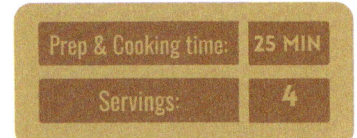

- 120g mayonnaise
- 5g Cajun seasoning
- 120g gluten-free panko bread crumbs
- One (450g) fillet cod, cut into four pieces
- cooking spray

Preperation

1. Put the breadcrumbs on a long platter and mix the may with Cajun in a little bowl.
2. Coat both sides of the fillets with the may mixture using a spoon and dredge them well in the breadcrumbs platter. Spray the fillets with cooking spray.
3. Place the fillets in both drawers of your Ninja Dual Zone Air Fryer and set it to the ROAST mode at 190°C, Set the time to fourteen mins.
4. Select the "MATCH" choice to apply the settings of the first zone to the second zone. Then press START/STOP to start.

36

Prep & Cooking time: 20 MIN
Servings: 4

Sausage Patties Recipe

Ingredients

- 300g fresh sausage patties

Preperation

1. First, you gotta preheat the Ninja Dual Zone Air Fryer to 200°C.
2. Add the patties to the drawers of your preheated machine.
3. AIR FRY for six mins choosing the "MATCH" setting.
4. Flip and cook for six additional min. Once it's done, place them on a paper towel-lined platter.

CHAPTER 3

STARTERS AND SIDES

Awesome Sweet and Spicy Roasted Carrots

Prep & Cooking time: 25 MIN
Servings: 2

Ingredients

- Cooking spray
- 15g butter, melted
- 15g hot honey
- 10g grated orange zest
- 2g ground cardamom
- 225g baby carrots
- 15ml freshly squeezed orange juice
- 1 pinch salt and ground black pepper

Preperation

1. Preheat your Ninja Dual Zone Air Fryer to 200°C. Grease its basket using a nonstick spray.
2. In a small bowl, place the butter, honey, orange zest, and cardamom and mix them, transfer a tbsp of the sauce to another small bowl and leave it there. In the first bowl add carrots and stir well to coat, then place the carrots in the drawer of your machine and fry them for about fifteen to twenty min.
3. Combine the juice of orange with the tbsp of sauce that you've transferred before to another bowl. Mix it well with carrots, season with salt, pepper, and serve.

Aubergine Parmesan Recipe

Prep & Cooking time: 35 MIN
Servings: 4

Ingredients

- 60g of breadcrumbs
- 60g Parmesan cheese (grated)
- 5g Italian seasoning
- 5g salt
- 2g dried basil
- 2g garlic powder
- 2g onion powder
- 2g freshly ground black pepper
- 30g flour
- 2 large eggs
- 1 medium aubergine, sliced into rounds
- 200g marinara sauce
- Mozzarella cheese

Preperation

1. Take three bowls, In the first bowl, put the flour. In the other one, add the eggs and beat them. In the last one, add the bread crumbs, and parmesan and mix them with Italian seasoning, salt, basil, garlic powder, onion powder, and black pepper.
2. Dunk the aubergine roundsin the first bowl, the second, and the last. Put them in a large dish and leave them for five minutes. Meanwhile, preheat your Ninja Dual Zone Air Fryer at 185°C.
3. Transfer the slices from the dish to the drawer of your machine, put them separated, Cook them for ten mins on the AIR FRY mode, flip and cook for five additional min. Add marinara and mozzarella over each slice. Put them again in your machine for one or two min. to melt the cheese. Serve!

Easy Pizza Dogs Recipe

Prep & Cooking time: 15 MIN
Servings: 2

Ingredients

- Two hot dogs
- 4 halved pepperoni slices
- 60g pizza sauce
- Two buns of hot dog
- 60g mozzarella cheese, shredded
- 10g olives, sliced

Preperation

1. First, preheat your Ninja Dual Zone Air Fryer to 200°C.
2. Next, using your knife, Slit the hot dogs (four slits on each one), put them in the drawer of the machine, and AIR FRY for three min. Once it's done, pull them out and directly to your cutting board.
3. Insert the halves of pepperoni in the slits you've made in the hot dogs (One in one). Then spread the sauce on the buns, add hot dogs, Sprinkle cheese, and olives.
4. Place the stuffed buns in the drawer and cook to melt the cheese for about two min.

Cannoli Recipe

Prep & Cooking time: 30 MIN
Servings: 8

Ingredients

- 680g Cottage Cheese
- 60g Icing sugar
- Zest from one orange
- 2g Sea salt
- 220g sugar (turbinado)
- Flour for the working board
- 1 (400g) pk. piecrusts
- White from on beaten egg
- 80g mini chocolate chips
- 60g roasted pistachios, chopped

Preperation

1. Strain the cheese from the excess liquid, then put it in a bowl, and add the Icing sugar, zest, and salt. put the mix into a piping bag or anything that can do the same job and leave it. On a platter, stir in the turbinado sugar and put it aside.
2. Sprinkle the flour on a working surface and roll the piecrusts on it, then split it into six-ten circles, and wrap them around cannoli moulds, Seal the edge with some of the egg white, then grease them all with the egg white. Dip them in the turbinado sugar.
3. Place them separated in both Ninja Dual Zone Air Fryer drawers.
4. Select DEHYDRATE function, and cook at 200°C for around seven mins.
5. Pull them out, cool for one min, then remove the cannoli mould. Leave them aside for ten mins.
6. Take two bowls, In the first one, put the chocolate chips, In the other, place the roasted pistachios. Put the cheese mixture that you've made in the first spet, into each cannoli shell. Dip 1 end in the first bowl and the other end in the second bowl. Drizzle some icing sugar. Enjoy!

Jalapeño Poppers Recipe

Prep & Cooking time: 30 MIN
Servings: 4

Ingredients

- 8 large jalapeño chiles
- 170g Cheddar cheese, shredded
- 120g cream cheese, softened
- 7g Sea salt, divided
- 60g plain flour
- 2 eggs, beaten
- 180g Breadcrumbs, very finely crushed
- 120g sour cream
- 10g lime zest
- Fresh juice 1 lime

Preperation

1. On a pan, pour 800ml of water and heat it over high, Place the jalapeños into that pan and cook for around three min.
2. Then, remove them to a cold water bowl to stay for a half-min. Take some paper towels and place them over a platter, and place the jalapeños on it. slit them vertically, remove the seeds, and dry the jalapeños well.
3. Take a bowl (no matter the size) and combine cheddar, cream cheese, and 2g of salt. Stuff each jalapeño with 1 tbsp of this mixture and seal the slits.
4. Take three bowls, In the first one, pour the eggs, In the other one, put the flour, and in the last one, mix breadcrumbs with the remaining salt. Dip the jalapeños in the first bowl, then in the flour, dip them again in the eggs, and coat them in the breadcrumbs.
5. Preheat your Ninja Dual Zone Air Fryer to 190°C for five mins.
6. Install the crisper plates in the drawers and spray them using cooking spray.
7. Divide the stuffed jalapeños between both prepared drawers.
8. Insert the drawers into the unit, set Zone 1 to AIR FRY and set the time to five mins.
9. Select the "MATCH" choice to apply the settings of the first zone to the second zone. Then press START/STOP to start, turning to both sides during cooking time.
10. In a serving bowl, mix sour cream, lime zest, and lime juice. Serve the jalapeños beside this bowl of cream.

Crispy Coconut Shrimp Recipe

Prep & Cooking time: 30 MIN
Servings: 4

Ingredients

- 60g plain flour
- 7g black pepper
- Two large eggs
- 65g unsweetened flaked coconut
- 80g breadcrumbs
- 340g peeled, deveined raw shrimp, tail-on
- 2g Sea salt
- 60g honey
- 60ml lime juice
- 1 serrano chile, thinly sliced

Preperation

1. Add flour to a large dish and mix it with pepper.
2. Crack and beat the eggs in a bowl.
3. In another dish, put the coconut and mix it with breadcrumbs.
4. Bring the shrimps and start dipping each of them, first in the flour, beaten eggs, and then in the breadcrumbs mixture. Grease them using a cooking spray.
5. Install the crisper plates in the drawers of your Ninja Dual Zone Air Fryer
6. Divide the shrimp between both prepared drawers, insert the drawers into the unit, set Zone 1 to AIR FRY at 200°C and set the time to eight mins.
7. Select the "MATCH" choice to apply the settings of the first zone to the second zone. Then press START/STOP to start, turning to both sides during cooking time. Sprinkle one gram of the salt over them.
8. Meanwhile, take a medium bowl, pour the lime juice, add honey, and serrano chile, and whisk them so you can have a sauce to serve with the shrimp.

Apple Pies Recipe

Prep & Cooking time: 45 MIN
Servings: 8

Ingredients

- 400g piecrusts
- 30g unsalted butter
- 360g apples, peeled and chopped
- 30g Light brown sugar
- 25g granulated sugar
- 1g ground cinnamon
- Flour, for the working board
- One beaten large egg
- 10g turbinado sugar

Preperation

1. Put the butter in a pan and melt it over medium. Once it's melted, add apples, granulated & light brown sugars, and cinnamon; cook with stirring for around eight min and then let it cool down.
2. Coat your working board with flour, spread the piecrusts on it, and cut the dough so you shape eight circles.
3. Stuff each circle with around two tbsps of apple mixture. Grease a side of each circle with some of the beaten eggs, Seal the dough circles. use a fork to curl the edge. Grease the top of each circle with beaten eggs, and drizzle some turbinado sugar.
4. Preheat your Ninja Dual Zone Air Fryer at 200°C for two mins
5. Divide the pies between both the Ninja drawers. Insert the drawers into the unit, set Zone 1 to BAKE and set the time to eight mins, turning to both sides during cooking time.
6. Select the "MATCH" choice to apply the settings of the first zone to the second zone. Then press START/STOP to start. Enjoy!

Tasty Churros Recipe

44

Prep & Cooking time: 45 MIN
Servings: 8

Ingredients

- 250ml water
- 15g unsalted butter
- 1g Sea salt
- 65g + 25g granulated sugar
- 120g plain flour
- 2 large eggs
- 3ml vanilla extract
- 5g ground cinnamon
- 30f unsalted butter, melted

Preperation

1. In your pan, pour the water and mix it with butter, salt, and 25g sugar over medium-high; stirring, until it boils. Stop the boiling, Pull the pan and add the flour and mix them.
2. Place the mixture in your stand mixer. beat it slowly for about two min. Crack the eggs on it, and mix to combine the eggs in the mixture. Add vanilla. Rise the mixing speed to medium, and mix to cool the combine for about eight min. Leave the dough for ten min, then, add it to a bag for pastry with a medium star tip.
3. Preheat the Ninja Dual Zone Air Fryer to 200°C. Coat the Ninja drawers using a cooking spray. Produce 10cm strips of the mixture from the pastry bag inside the drawers. Spray the top of each strip.
4. Insert the drawers inside, set Zone 1 to DEHYDRATE and set the time to eight mins, turning to both sides during cooking time.
5. Select the "MATCH" choice to apply the settings of the first zone to the second zone. Then press START/STOP to start.
6. Mix cinnamon with the rest of the sugar in a small bowl, Grease each strip with the melted butter and dip it in that bowl of cinnamon. Serve.

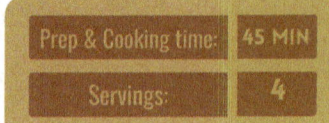

Mozzarella Sticks Recipe

45

Prep & Cooking time: 45 MIN
Servings: 4

Ingredients

- 60g plain flour
- 5g Bicarbonate of soda
- Two large eggs
- 15ml whole milk
- 120g seasoned breadcrumbs
- Eight mozzarella string cheese sticks
- 120g marinara sauce

Preperation

1. Add flour to a large dish and mix it with bicarbonate of soda. Put two small bowls in front of you, beat the eggs with milk in one, and add the breadcrumbs in the other. Dip the mozzarella sticks in the first dish of flour, then in the bowl of milk and eggs; and dip in the last bowl. Freeze the sticks for a half-hour.
2. Coat the drawers of your machine using the cooking spray.
3. Place half of the sticks in the first drawer and the other half in the second.
4. Insert the drawers into the unit, set Zone 1 to AIR FRY at 200°C and set the time to six mins.
5. Select the "MATCH" choice to apply the settings of the first zone to the second zone. Then press START/STOP to start.

Easy Baked Pineapple Recipe

Prep & Cooking time: 1 HR
Servings: 6

Ingredients

- 200g white sugar
- 110g butter, softened
- Four eggs, beaten
- 520g pineapple
- Five bread slices; Broken into crumbs

Preperation

1. First, you gotta preheat the Ninja Dual Zone Air Fryer to 175°C.
2. Place the sugar in a mixing bowl and combine it well with butter, then add the beaten eggs and mix, add drained pineapple then the breadcrumbs, and mix.
3. Place this combine in a baking dish that fits with the drawer of your Ninja Dual Zone Air Fryer.
4. Insert the dish into the machine, choose BAKE, set teh time to sixty mins and press START/STOP to start.

Tasty Potato Wedges

47

Prep & Cooking time: 35 MIN
Servings: 4

Ingredients

- Two russet potatoes, cut into wedges
- 20ml olive oil
- 2g paprika
- 2g parsley flakes
- 2g chili powder
- 3g sea salt
- 1g ground black pepper

Preperation

1. In a bowl, put the potato pieces, and pour oil over them, then add paprika, parsley, chilli, salt, and pepper and stir to combine them.
2. Now, preheat your Ninja Dual Zone Air Fryer to 200°C.
3. Insert the potatoes in the drawer, and cook on the AIR FRY mode for ten mins. Then flip them and cook for five min more. Enjoy!

Delicious Stuffed Mushrooms Recipe

Prep & Cooking time: 35 MIN
Servings: 6

Ingredients

- 450g white button mushrooms (cleaned and stems removed)
- Two Spring onions
- 120g cream cheese, softened
- 30g Cheddar cheese shredded
- 1g ground paprika
- A pinch of salt
- cooking spray

Preperation

1. Chop and mince the spring onions and detach white and green leaves, Now, Preheat your Ninja Dual Zone Air Fryer to 180°C.
2. In a large bowl, place the white leaves of spring onions, cream cheese, and cheddar cheese and mix them well after adding paprika, and salt. Fill the mushrooms with the mixture deeply.
3. Place the mushrooms in your machine's both drawers after you spray them.
4. Insert the drawers into the unit, set Zone 1 to AIR FRY and set the time to eight mins.
5. Select the "MATCH" choice to apply the settings of the first zone to the second zone. Then press START/STOP to start.
6. Drizzle scallion green leaves over the mushrooms, Serve after five mins.

49

Prep & Cooking time: 20 MIN
Servings: 8

Roasted Almonds Starter

Ingredients

- 180ml hot water
- 4g Pink salt
- 280g raw almonds
- 15ml olive oil
- salt to taste

Preperation

1. First, preheat your Ninja Dual Zone Air Fryer to 175°C, Cover a pan that fits in the machine with aluminium foil. In a small bowl, pour the water and add the pink salt, mix well to get dissolved.
2. Put the almonds in a stainless medium bowl and pour the dissolved pink salt you've just made over the almonds; stir well to grease them. Transfer the almonds to the pan you've already covered with aluminium foil.
3. Insert the pan into the drawer of your Ninja Dual Zone Air Fryer, Set it to ROAST and cook for seven mins.
4. Pull out the drawer, stir, and place it inside again; cook until brown, around five to six additional min. When it's done, place the almonds in a medium bowl, pour oil over them, add salt as desired, and mix well to combine. Serve them cold.

Spicy Wings

Prep & Cooking time: 30 MIN
Servings: 2

Ingredients

- 680g chicken wings and drummettes
- 10ml olive oil
- 8g smoked paprika
- 8g chilli powder
- 4g ground cumin
- 5g onion powder
- 5g garlic powder
- 4g ground black pepper
- 5g Sea salt
- 5g cayenne pepper

Preperation

1. Put the chicken in a wide bowl, pour oil, and mix them. In another bowl, mix the remaining ingredients. Sprinkle chicken with this mixture and mix it.
2. Preheat your Ninja Dual Zone Air Fryer to 190°.
3. Insert the chicken into your preheated machine's drawer and cook for around twelve mins on the AIR FRY function, turning to both sides during the cooking time.
4. Raise the heat to 200°C and cook for two to three additional min to crispier the wings. Serving after a few mins.

51

Prep & Cooking time: 15 MIN
Servings: 2

Awesome Lemon Pepper Shrimp Recipe

Ingredients

- 15ml olive oil
- Lime juiced from 1 lemon
- 3g lemon pepper
- 2g paprika
- 2g garlic powder
- 340g medium shrimps, peeled and deveined
- One lemon, sliced

Preperation

1. First, preheat your Ninja Dual Zone Air Fryer to 200°C.
2. In a mixing bowl, mix all ingredients, then add the shrimp and mix it well with other ingredients.
3. Transfer the shrimps to your machine's drawer. Select AIR FRY and set the time to eight mins. Garnish with lemon slices and serve.

Prep & Cooking time: 40 MIN
Servings: 4

Easy Spicy Runner Beans Recipe

Ingredients

- 340g fresh runner beans, trimmed
- 15ml sesame oil
- 5ml soy sauce
- 5ml lime juice
- One clove of garlic, minced
- 3g red pepper flakes

Preperation

1. First, preheat your Ninja Dual Zone Air Fryer to 200°C.
2. In a mixing bowl, whisk all ingredients, then add the runner beans and toss well to coat with other ingredients. Leave it to marinate for about five min.
3. Divide the green beans between the drawers of your Ninja Dual Zone Air Fryer.
4. Insert the drawers into the unit, set Zone 1 to DEHYDRATE and set the time to twelve mins.
5. Select the "MATCH" choice to apply the settings of the first zone to the second zone. Then press START/STOP to start, shaking them a few times during that. Serve!

Rosemary Potato Wedges Recipe

Prep & Cooking time: 30 MIN
Servings: 4

Ingredients

- Two large russet potatoes, sliced into wedges
- 15ml extra-virgin olive oil
- 10g seasoned salt
- 5g chopped fresh rosemary

Preperation

1. As a first step, preheat your Ninja Dual Zone Air Fryer to 190°C.
2. Mix potatoes with the remaining ingredients in a mixing bowl and toss well.
3. Then transfer them to the drawers of both zones.
4. Insert the drawers into the unit, set Zone 1 to AIR FRY and set the time to ten mins.
5. Select the "MATCH" choice to apply the settings of the first zone to the second zone. Then press START/STOP to start, flip them and cook for ten additional min.

Roasted Asparagus Side Dish

Prep & Cooking time: 20 MIN
Servings: 2

Ingredients

- One bunch of fresh asparagus, trimmed
- A cooking spray of avocado oil
- 2g garlic powder
- 2g pink salt
- 1g ground peppercorns
- 1g red pepper flakes
- 60g Parmesan cheese, grated

Preperation

1. First, you have to preheat your Ninja Dual Zone Air Fryer to 190°C, Coat the drawer using parchment paper.
2. Put the asparagus in the coated drawer of your machine and spray it with avocado oil. Add the remaining ingredients and cheese over them.
3. Select ROAST and set the time to nine mins, then press START/STOP to start.

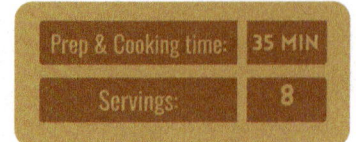

Crispy Donut Sticks

Prep & Cooking time: 35 MIN
Servings: 8

Ingredients

- 1 (225g) pkg crescent roll dough
- 60g butter, melted
- 100g white sugar
- 5g ground cinnamon
- 150g any flavor fruit jam

Preperation

1. Spread the dough on a working surface and pat it out to a medium rectangle. Then split it in half, and cut them into sticks. Dredge the sticks in the melted butter and put them in the drawer of your Ninja Dual Zone Air Fryer.
2. Select MAX CRISP at 195°C and set the time to five mins, then press START/STOP to start.
3. In a medium bowl, add sugar and mix it with cinnamon. Dredge the cooked sticks in the mixture while they are hot. Serve them beside your chosen jam.

Crispy Truffle Fries Recipe

Prep & Cooking time: 1 HR
Servings: 4

Ingredients

- 800g russet potatoes, peeled and cut into fries
- 30ml truffle-infused olive oil
- 2g paprika
- 15g Parmesan cheese, grated
- 3g fresh parsley, chopped
- 5g black truffle sea salt

Preperation

1. Put the fries in a large bowl. Pout water over them until they get covered, and leave them like that for thirty min. Drain and pat dry.
2. Next, preheat your Ninja Dual Zone Air Fryer to 200°C. Drain the potatoes, dry them, then transfer them to another bowl, pour oil, and paprika, and mix them with the potatoes.
3. Install the crisper plate in the drawer and place the potatoes into it, insert the drawer into the unit and cook on AIR FRY for twenty mins, shaking 4 separate times during that. Once it's done, put them in a bowl. Sprinkle cheese, parsley, and salt. over them and toss well.

Asparagus Fries Recipe

Prep & Cooking time: 20 MIN
Servings: 6

Ingredients

- One large egg
- 5g honey
- 120g panko breadcrumbs
- 120g Parmesan cheese, grated
- Twelve asparagus spears, trimmed
- 40g stone-ground mustard
- 60g Greek yogurt

Preperation

1. As a first step, preheat your Ninja Dual Zone Air Fryer to 200°C, Take two bowls, and mix the egg with honey in a bowl. and mix breadcrumbs with cheese on another one. Dredge the asparagus in the first mixture, then in the breadcrumbs mixture.
2. Install the crisper plate in the Ninja drawers, Divide the asparagus between the drawers and insert them into the unit.
3. Set Zone 1 to AIR FRY and set the time to six mins. Select the "MATCH" choice to apply the settings of the first zone to the second zone. Then press START/STOP to start.
4. Mix the other ingredients you still have in a small bowl to have a dipping sauce.

Crispy Avocado Fries Recipe

Prep & Cooking time: 20 MIN
Servings: 2

Ingredients

- 30g plain flour
- 1g ground black pepper
- 1g salt
- One egg
- 5ml water
- One ripe avocado, halved, seeded, peeled, and sliced
- 60g breadcrumbs
- cooking spray

Preperation

1. Preheat your Ninja Dual Zone Air Fryer to 200°C, Take three small bowls, place flour and combine it with pepper, and salt in the first bowl. Whisk the egg & water in the second bowl and put the breadcrumbs in the remaining bowl.
2. Coat the avocado slices with the flour mixture, Dip them in the second bowl and roll them to the breadcrumbs.
3. Install the crisper plate in the drawer and place the slices into it, Spray them on both sides.
4. Select AIR FRY and set the time to four mins. Turn and cook for three additional min.

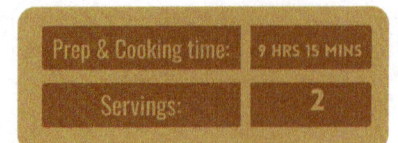

Delicious Corn Nuts Recipe

Prep & Cooking time: 9 HRS 15 MINS
Servings: 2

Ingredients

- 250g giant white corn
- 45ml vegetable oil
- 7g salt

Preperation

1. In a wide bowl, put the corn, pour water over until the corn is covered, and leave it like that overnight.
2. Discard the water and dry the corn and leave it in the air for twenty min. Then, preheat your Ninja Dual Zone Air Fryer to 200°C.
3. Mix the corn with oil and salt in a bowl and stir, Transfer it to the drawer of your preheated machine.
4. Choose DEHYDRATE, set teh time to ten mins and press START/STOP to start, Then shake and cook again for ten mins. Shake it one more time and cook for five further mins.
5. Place the cooked corn on a towel-lined platter and let them cool for twenty mins before serving.

Enjoyable Roasted Bananas

Prep & Cooking time: 9 MIN
Servings: 1

Ingredients

- One banana, sliced into thick rounds
- Cooking spray (Avocado oil)

Preperation

1. At the beginning, preheat your Ninja Dual Zone Air Fryer to 190°C and put a perforated parchment round in the bottom of your machine's drawer.
2. Add slices separated to the prepared drawer and coat with the cooking spray.
3. Select ROAST, set the time to fifteen mins, and then press START/STOP to start. Flip the slices and cook for two to three mins more.

Easy Spicy Roasted Peanuts Recipe

Prep & Cooking time: 30 MIN
Servings: 8

Ingredients

- 30ml olive oil
- 10g seafood seasoning
- 1g cayenne pepper
- 140g raw Spanish peanuts
- salt to taste

Preperation

1. As a first step, preheat your Ninja Dual Zone Air Fryer to 160°C, Mix oil with seasoning and pepper in a wide bowl. Put the peanuts in the mixture and stir to coat.
2. Place peanuts in the drawer of your machine and select ROAST, set the time to ten mins, and then press START/STOP to start. Toss and keep cooking for ten min more.
3. Add salt to them and toss. Cook for five min more. Place on a paper towel-lined platter to cool.

Thank You

Printed in Great Britain
by Amazon